Jolie and the Change of Heart

By Adriana Suyama

For *Chris, Jayden, Eli, IslaLou,* and *CharlieAnne*

Some extra special thanks...

Chrissy Reyes, this dream would not even have begun had it not been for you. Thank you for navigating this journey for me, for never tiring of my endless questions, and for planting the roots for this flyaway dreamer.

Thais Eliasen, thank you for working on each and every tiny detail that goes into publishing a book. Thank you for making my dream a reality. When you've got big dreams you need someone on your side who, not only dreams big with you, but believes in the dream, pushes you through the fear, and who is on fire for what you can accomplish. Thank you Thais for being that for me and for this dream.

Sarah Momo Romero and *Kyla Vaughn,* a huge thank you for your incredible insight and for taking the time to encourage and help me tell my story.

© Copyright 2020

Deep, deep down in a secret part of the ocean was a city called Elysia.

In Elysia lived a famous and beautiful mermaid named Jolie.

Jolie may have been beautiful on the outside, but her heart was ugly. Jolie was unkind to the kids at school, and she would not play with anyone she thought was different from her.

Jolie only thought about herself and today was no different. As she swam home from school with her grandma, she became lost in her own thoughts. She slipped and fell right into some mucky sludge!

She looked down at her hands to wipe them off and realized they were covered in muck! "What..." she exclaimed. "What is this?"
Not only that, but it was all over her arms, her face, and her beautiful tail!
She grabbed some moss and tried to scrub it off, but it would not come off.

Jolie looked up at her grandma. "Grandma!" Jolie pouted. "Help me! Why won't it come off! Just look at my beautiful tail!" Jolie burst into tears.

"I think I know what's happening. You tease your friends and you are unkind to those around you. You are such a beautiful girl, but your heart has turned ugly. And now the mud is sticking to you. It won't come off until you change your heart."

Jolie's eyes got big and wide.
"What!" she shrieked. "That's not fair! Well..." Jolie huffed.
"You're wrong! My mom will get this off. You'll see!"

"Suit yourself," her grandma sighed. "But it's this kind of attitude that got you into this mess." Jolie stopped and thought about that for a minute, but then she turned on her fin and swam home ahead of her grandma.

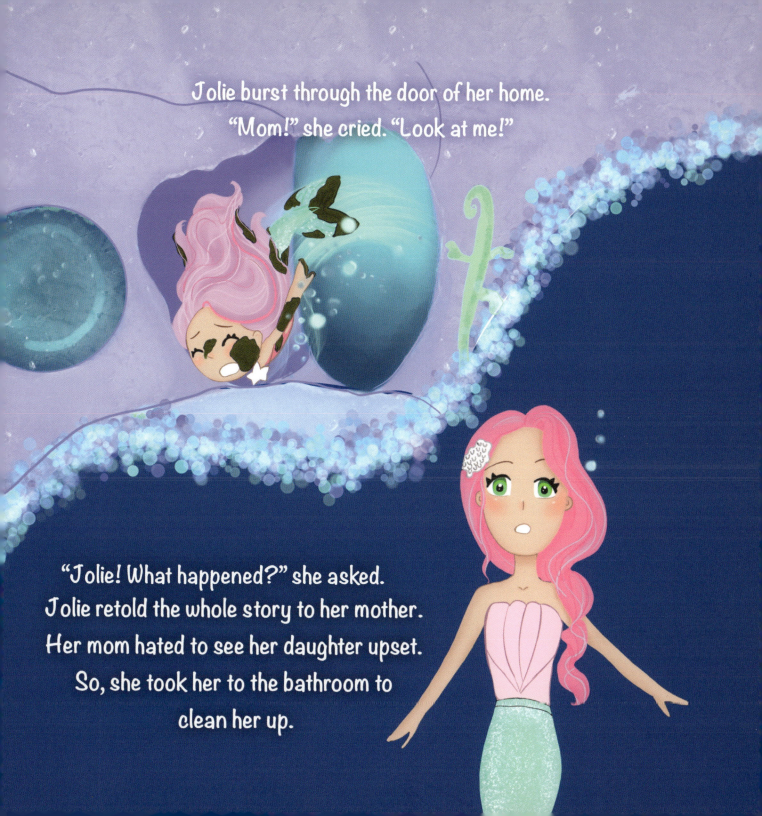

Jolie burst through the door of her home.
"Mom!" she cried. "Look at me!"

"Jolie! What happened?" she asked.
Jolie retold the whole story to her mother.
Her mom hated to see her daughter upset.
So, she took her to the bathroom to
clean her up.

Her mom tried different soaps,

and different sponges,

but still...it would not come off. And all the while, Jolie cried and cried.

"Well...I'm out of ideas," her mother said.
"We'll just have to wait and see if it comes off on it's own."
"What?" Jolie sniffed. "I can't go to school like this!"
"I'm sorry, starfish. There's nothing I can do."

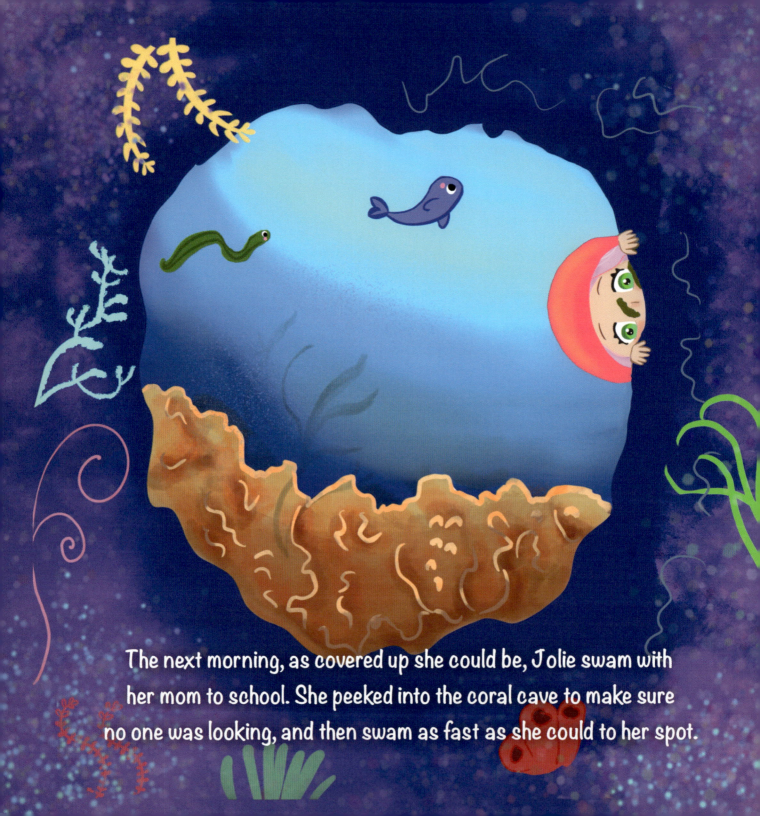

The next morning, as covered up she could be, Jolie swam with her mom to school. She peeked into the coral cave to make sure no one was looking, and then swam as fast as she could to her spot.

Her friend Charlotte spotted her and swam over to where she sat. "What are you wearing Jolie?" she giggled.

"Sshh!" Jolie scolded. "None of your business!"
The teacher swam in just then and asked everyone to sit down.

Jolie popped up and shouted, "Stop staring at me!" but no one listened.
Tears ran down her face and she swished right out of class.

The next few days were miserable. Jolie wouldn't play or talk to anyone, and the kids kept whispering and staring at her.

As Jolie sat alone on a rock one day, a little girl nearby was crying. "Do you mind?!" Jolie said. "Can't you see I have my own problems?!" "I lost my bracelet," she blubbered. "My mom gave it to me, and I can't find it anywhere." Jolie hmphed. "Well, if I help you find it, will you go away?"

The little girl flitted off happy as can be, but Jolie sat back down. She looked down at her hands and noticed a small bit of the muck was gone!
Was the muck going away because I helped the little girl?
Jolie wondered.

Jolie popped up, excited at the idea, and wanted to try it out.

As the days went on, Jolie noticed when others needed help with something.

And she realized that not only did her spots go away, but...

she felt happier inside when she was helping people.

She helped....

and helped...

and helped some more.

When Jolie had just one spot left, she went to see her grandma. Her grandma said, "Jolie I'm so proud of you. You look so happy!"

"I am happy, Grandma! I love helping people!"

Grandma smiled at Jolie and pointed at her hand.
The last spot was vanishing before their eyes!
"Now you truly are the most beautiful girl, inside and out."

Surprise! Time for some fun! Color Jolie, Grandma & Shelby.

How would you look as a mermaid?

Author

Adriana Suyama is a first-time author and full-time homeschooling mom of four. As a child she grew up spending endless hours imagining and reading and enjoying being lost in the stories. As a young adult she worked and volunteered with kids with special needs and found immeasurable joy in children of all kinds. As she became a mom, that joy fueled her desire to become an author.

Illustrator

Janelle Jordan is an artist from California. She was homeschooled with her four siblings, and has loved drawing since she was little. This is her first time illustrating for a picture book. A dream come true! She wants to encourage you to go for your dreams! She is honored to illustrate for Adriana, a talented author with a passion for kids and incredible stories to share. If you love this story, you will enjoy her future books!